217

MW01139502

This book belongs to

Hazel Ann

Given by *With Love*

Mamma

Little Acts of Grace

of

Grace

Rosemarie Gortler & Donna Piscitelli
Illustrated by Mimi Sternhagen

Our Sunday Visitor Publishing Division
Our Sunday Visitor, Inc.
Huntington, Indiana 46750

Nihil Obstat: Rev. Paul F. deLadurantaye, S.T.D.
Censor Librorum

Imprimatur: Most Reverend Paul S. Loverde
Bishop of Arlington
October 22, 2001

The *nihil obstat* and *imprimatur* are official declarations that a book or pamphlet is free of doctrinal or moral error. No implication is contained therein that those who have granted the *nihil obstat* and *imprimatur* agree with the contents, opinions, or statements expressed.

Our Sunday Visitor Publishing Division
Our Sunday Visitor, Inc.
200 Noll Plaza
Huntington, IN 46750

ISBN: 978-0-97077-567-2 (Inventory No. T3)

Cover design by Monica Haneline
Cover and interior art by Mimi Sternhagen
Interior design by Sherri L. Hoffman

PRINTED IN THE UNITED STATES OF AMERICA

Contents

6

Introduction

It's the *little* things that we do that show love and affection:

- 💜 a wink
- 💜 a touch
- 💜 a smile
- 💜 a glance
- 💜 a thank you

It's waving at someone, just because . . .

Little things say "I love you" louder than shouting from a mountaintop.

To God, *little* things mean a lot, too.

"Well done, good and faithful servant;
you have been faithful over a little, I will set
you over much." (Matthew 25:21 – RSV)

Sometimes a *little* thing takes no more time than snapping your fingers.

The *little* things that say
    "I love you"
can be done many times during the day.

Sometimes just changing the *little* things we do helps build our friendship with God.

Friends need to be in touch.

"You are my friends if you do what I command you.
I no longer call you slaves. . . . I have called you
friends." (John 15:14-15 – NAB)

Little Acts of Grace
for Jesus and His Church

Bowing Your Head

The Bible says that when someone mentions
    the name of
      Jesus,
everyone in Heaven bows.

We on Earth sometimes forget that
    Jesus
is a holy name.

Bowing our heads when someone says His name is a
little gesture that gives
    love and
        respect to
           Jesus.

A *little* nod of the head is a great sign of respect.

He would like that a lot.

Therefore God also highly exalted [Jesus]
and gave him the name that is above every name.
(Philippians 2:9 – NRSV)

Passing a Church

Ever pass a Catholic church on your way somewhere?
Remember the tabernacle inside?
Who is in that tabernacle?

Jesus, of course, and He loves to hear from us.

When we pass a Catholic church, we can talk to Him,
if only in a *little* secret whisper or a thought:

"Jesus, I love You"
      or
"Jesus and Mary, I love you both. Save souls"
      or even
"Hi, Jesus."

Whatever you say,
bow your head,
or tip your hat as a sign of affection
as you pass the church
because Jesus is inside.

It's a *little* thing . . . and
He would love for you to acknowledge Him.

"And behold, I am with you always, until the end
of the age." (Matthew 28:20 – NAB)

Dressing for Church

Would you wear a bathing suit
to go see the president of the United States?

Sounds funny, huh?

Would you wear shorts and a tee shirt
to go see a king?

That would be silly!

How do you dress to go see Christ the King?

It would be such a *nice little thing* if we made sure our clothes were clean, comfortable, and *modest* when we visit Our Lord.

"When the Son of Man comes in his glory, and all the angels with him, he will sit upon his glorious throne, and all the nations will be assembled before him."
(Matthew 25:31 – NAB)

Using Holy Water

Beside the front door of every Catholic church is a "dish" with water in it.

Have you ever noticed it?

It is a holy water font,
and the water is special water,
blessed by a priest.

As we go into the church, we dip our fingertips into the water and make the Sign of the Cross.

Why do we do this?

To prepare ourselves to be in God's presence,
we bless ourselves as we were blessed in Baptism.

We prepare ourselves to visit every important person. So we prepare ourselves to visit God.

He appreciates this *little* thoughtfulness.

The Lord spoke to Moses, saying: Take the
Levites from among the Israelites and cleanse
them. Thus you shall do to them, to cleanse them:
sprinkle the water of purification on them.
(Numbers 8:5-7 – NRSV)

18

Making the Sign of the Cross

Sometimes when people rush to make the
Sign of the Cross,
they look as if they are
fanning themselves,
swatting mosquitoes,
or shooing flies.

God might be wondering what they are doing.

When we make the Sign of the Cross,
it is important to draw a cross
with your right hand,
from your forehead,
to your chest,
and to each shoulder.

The Sign of the Cross is a little prayer of love:

> **In the name of the Father,**
> **and of the Son,**
> **and of the Holy Spirit.**
> **Amen.**

"Go therefore and make disciples of all nations,
baptizing them in the name of the Father and
of the Son and of the Holy Spirit."
(Matthew 28:19 – RSV)

Genuflecting

We kneel on one knee before entering a pew in a Catholic Church.

Isn't that a funny thing to do?

Not really.

It's how we genuflect. That means we kneel to adore Christ in the tabernacle.

Some people think we are bowing to the crucifix or to a statue.

But we aren't.

We are bowing to the living presence of Christ in the tabernacle.

Genuflecting when you go into a pew
in a Catholic church
is a *little* way of saying
"I know You are here, Jesus."

At the name of Jesus every knee should bend, of those in heaven and on earth and under the earth.
(Philippians 2:10 – NAB)

Little Acts of Grace
at Mass

Distractions

Sometimes at Mass,
when our minds and hearts should be on prayer,
our minds wander.

We think about other things:
where we are going or
what our friends are doing.
This can happen a lot.
It happens to kids, to parents, and to every single
one of us.

God does understand!

BUT He wants us to bring our minds and hearts back to
prayer quickly.

We can do a wonderful *little* thing by politely saying,
"Excuse me, Lord, for wandering."

Then we bring our minds back to prayer.
It would mean so much!

And you know, He will take care of our distractions.

Pray without ceasing.
(1 Thessalonians 5:17 – NAB)

'Lord, Have Mercy'

Did you ever notice that at Mass we say a *little* prayer?

Lord, have mercy.
Christ, have mercy.
Lord, have mercy.

Why do we do that?

You see, Jesus tells us that we can count on His mercy if we only ask for it.

He knows we make mistakes.
He wants us to be humble and ask for His mercy.

Do you know why?
Because He loves you
and me
and all of us.

So the next time you are at Mass,
pay attention to this *little* prayer.

It is an important *little* prayer.

"The tax collector stood off at a distance and would not even raise his eyes to heaven but beat his breast and prayed, 'O God, be merciful to me a sinner.' I tell you, [he] went home justified."
(Luke 18:13-14 – NAB)

The Prayer Before the Gospel

Did you ever wonder why people seem to
scratch their foreheads, itch their noses,
and rub their chests before the Gospel?

Why do they do that?
Well, they aren't itching, scratching, or rubbing.
They are making the Sign of the Cross on the head,
on the lips, and over the heart.

The Gospel is so important that we stand to hear that
story.

Then we especially focus our minds and hearts to hear
what Jesus said.

When we make these *little* crosses, we say a *little* prayer:

**May the Lord be
in my mind,
on my lips,
and in my heart.**

Then our minds and hearts are open to hear the Word
of God.

"You shall love the Lord, your God, with all your
heart, with all your soul, and with all your mind.
This is the greatest and the first commandment."
(Matthew 22:37-38 – NAB)

27

The Consecration

It's right in the middle of Mass.
And the most important and exciting part is happening!

Angels are bowing low as the priest lifts up the host and the cup of wine.

It's the Consecration.

The bread and wine are changing into the Body and Blood of Christ.

It is such a solemn and important part of the Mass.

And the *biggest* thing we can do at Mass is to thank Jesus for coming to us in this wonderful way.

Jesus took bread, and blessed, and broke it, and gave it to the disciples and said, "Take, eat; this is my body." And he took a cup, and when he had given thanks he gave it to them, saying, "Drink of it, all of you; for this is my blood of the covenant, which is poured out for many for the forgiveness of sins."
(Matthew 26:26-28 – RSV)

Communion

It's Communion time!
It's time to receive Jesus into our hearts.

We walk down the aisle,
our hands folded in prayer,
our heads bowed,
getting ready to receive Jesus.

It's important not to swing our arms or look around.

And we *never chew gum* at Mass.

Little things like folding our hands
and bowing our heads
help us think about Jesus.

And that *makes Him happy.*

"I am the living bread which came down from
heaven; if any one eats of this bread, he will live
for ever; and the bread which I shall give for the
life of the world is my flesh." (John 6:51 – RSV)

Whenever we receive Communion,
we receive the Body and Blood of Jesus.

This is when we are very close to Our Lord.
He becomes food for us.

When we receive Communion,
We concentrate on how we *love* Him.
And we pray to Him.

We give Him all our problems.
We can pray for people we love.

He listens all the time.
And He is very near us
when we receive Communion.

Jesus said to them, "I am the bread of life; whoever
comes to me will never hunger, and whoever believes
in me will never thirst." (John 6:35 – NAB)

Little Acts of Grace
in Prayer

Praying to Mary

Did you ever notice the statue of Mary in church?

Did you notice that the statue sometimes has flowers or candles in front of it?

Catholics are devoted to Our Blessed Mother because she is the Mother of God and our Mother.

She is the Queen of Heaven and Earth.

When we pray to Mary, we ask her to pray to God for us. We say:

**Hail Mary, full of grace,
the Lord is with thee.
Blessed art thou among women,
and blessed is the fruit
of thy womb, Jesus.**

**Holy Mary, Mother of God,
pray for us sinners,
now and at the hour of our death.
Amen.**

A great sign appeared in the sky, a woman
clothed with the sun, with the moon under her feet,
and on her head a crown of twelve stars.
(Revelation 12:1 – NAB)

Praying to the Saints

There are so many good people in Heaven.
We call them saints.

All the saints were once living on Earth.
They remember what it is like
    to be sad,
        to be happy,
            to be silly.

We can ask the saints to pray for us
— just as we ask our family to pray for us
or our friends to pray for us.

It is good to pray to the saints.
Because they are in Heaven,
they are already close to God.
And He listens to them.

You can start by praying to the saint you were named
after or to a favorite saint.

This is a *little* thing we can do
to get closer to God.

"Be perfect, just as your heavenly Father is perfect."
(Matthew 5:48 – NAB)

Praying to the Angels

Angel of God, my guardian dear,
to whom God's love commits me here,
ever this day be at my side,
to light and guard,
to rule and guide.
Amen.

You have an angel who is with you.
All day, all night, always.
Your angel is with you when you are
lonely, sad, angry, or scared.
Your angel is with you
even when you are happy.

We all have angels who guard us.
They are our guardian angels.

Saying this *little* prayer is a *little* way
of thanking our angels.

"See that you do not despise one of these little
ones; for I tell you that in heaven their angels always
behold the face of my Father who is in heaven."
(Matthew 18:10 – RSV)

Praying for the Sick

The flashing lights and squealing siren
of an ambulance are very scary,
aren't they?

Do you wonder who is in that ambulance?
Do you wonder about his family?
Do you wonder if he is okay?

Instead of wondering, you can do something.

Say a quick *little* prayer for the person in the ambulance.
Ask God to grant healing, peace, and comfort to the
sick, and wisdom to the doctor.

When we pray for one another, God hears us.
He always listens.

Praying for the sick is a wonderful *little* thing we can do.

Pray in the Spirit at all times in every prayer
and supplication. (Ephesians 6:18 – NRSV)

Praying at Mealtime

**Bless us, O Lord,
and these Thy gifts,
which we are about to receive
from Thy bounty,
through Christ our Lord.
Amen.**

This is the prayer Catholics say
before we eat our meals.

Isn't that wonderful? A prayer that we all say!

We ask the Lord to bless us
and the food we are about to eat.
And we thank Him for giving us all we have.

This is a *little* thing that means so much.
How often do we remember
to thank the Lord
during the day?

He likes it when we say, "Thank You."

"In all circumstances, give thanks, for this is
the will of God for you in Christ Jesus."
(1 Thessalonians 5:18 – NAB)

Praying at Bedtime

Every night,
    before we go to bed,
        we kneel and pray.

Some people pray the Our Father and the Hail Mary.

Some people just talk to Jesus.
They tell Him about their day,
    ask forgiveness for their sins,
        and thank Him for His graces.

What is important
is that we pray *every night*
before we go to bed.

And getting on your knees when you pray tells Jesus
that you *know* He is God.

This is a *little* thing that means a lot to Our Lord.

"When you pray, go to your inner room, close
the door, and pray to your Father in secret."
(Matthew 6:6 – NAB)

Final Note

Our faith is filled with lots of *little* things that show our love and affection for God.

It's the *little* things that mean a lot.
The celebration of the Mass is the most important prayer of all.

But the *little* things we do every day to praise and love God help keep our minds and hearts focused on Him.

So *little* things do mean a lot!

I will praise you, LORD, with all my heart;
I will declare all your wondrous deeds.
(Psalm 9:2 – NAB)

About the Authors and Illustrator

Rosemarie Gorter is an R.N. and a licensed professional counselor. She is also an extraordinary minister of the Eucharist, a member of the Secular Franciscan Order, and a volunteer for Project Rachel. Rosemarie and her husband, Fred, have five children and nineteen grandchildren.

Donna Piscitelli is is a school administrator in Fairfax, Virginia. She is active in her church and in Christian outreach. She and her husband, Stephen, have four children and ten grandchildren.

Mimi Sternhagen is a home-school teacher and mother of five children. She and her husband, Don, assist with Family Life ministry in their parish. In addition to her collaborated works with Rosemarie and Donna, Mimi has illustrated *Catholic Cardlinks: Patron Saints* and *Teach Me About Mary*.

The authors extend a special thank-you to Father Francis Peffley, who selected the Scripture passages used in this book. Father Peffley is pastor of Holy Trinity Parish, Gainesville, Virginia.